This book is for you if...

- you have always wondered about what running your own business would be like.

- you are prepared to admit you don't know what you don't know.

- you wonder whether you have personally "got what it takes".

- you think you have an idea but you don't know whether it is commercially viable.

- you are unsure what business skills you will need.

- you don't know what a business plan needs to look like.

- you don't know where to start in terms of raising money.

- you have heard of marketing but are not entirely sure what it is and why you would need it.

- you find the idea of selling scary or daunting.

- you want to put the odds in your favour so that if you do decide to start a business, it will be successful.

What people are saying

"Having read 'From Crew to Captain' almost 2 years ago, I have since been privileged to work with David through the founding stages of launching my own new business venture. At the time of writing this, I find myself literally 1 week away from the official launch of a business which I know is so much better equipped for success having had David's incredible guidance, support and nuggets of inspiration. Whilst others have come and gone, 'From Crew to Captain' continues to have a well earned place on my desk, it's pages well worn with many margin notes and sticky labels protruding - a sure sign of an extremely valuable resource of any budding entrepreneur - and I await his next chapter, which I am sure will be equally insightful and well timed as I hope my business moves into its next phase.

Lisa Thompson - Managing Director, Blue Acorns Ltd

What I love about 'From Crew to Captain' is that it is written for people leaving corporate life to set up in business by someone who has done just that. What's even better is that David does not simply assume that one size fits all but uses all of his experience to provide a framework - rather than a rigid formula - for business success. I left 'corporate' life nearly 8 years before this book was published and yet it is just as relevant today, if not more so, as it would have been when I probably needed it most! I recommend it to all my clients, regardless of experience.

Gordon Borer - Exceptional Performers

I met David Mellor when, after more than 30 years in corporate life, the opportunity arose at age 50 to embark on a new career...

David opened my mind to the idea of a portfolio career, one in which I could pursue the topics of business that both interested me, and where I could also use my knowledge and insights to add value to others...

My getting to know David coincided with the publication of 'From Crew to Captain' and when I first read the book, I felt that its content had been written specifically for me – almost every page resonated with my own experience. The practical tips and useful diagnostics, together with the simple to understand charts and diagrams, all proved to be an invaluable source of reference.

Paul Plant - Founder & Principal, Radicle Consulting Ltd

About the Author

Since 2001, David has developed a portfolio of activities which derive principally from 25 years' experience in commercial and investment banking with HSBC and Deutsche Bank. His consultancy activities embrace strategic planning and implementation, and mentoring existing and aspiring entrepreneurs. He is a recognised expert in his field, regularly speaking at conferences and running seminars and workshops. He provides one-on-one and group mentoring to aspiring entrepreneurs, many of whom are aiming to establish themselves as consultants.

He published *From Crew to Captain* in 2010, written for people making the transition from working for big institutions to working for themselves. He has followed that up by launching *From Crew to Captain: A Privateer's Tale* in 2014, which is written for people establishing consultancy practices.

The third book in the trilogy, *From Crew to Captain: Commander of the Fleet*, was released in November 2015 and addresses the "growing pains" issues faced by successful start-ups. He is also co-author of FT Publishing's *Inspirational Gamechangers* which launched in 2015.

He is an Honorary Senior Visiting Fellow in the Faculty of Finance at Cass Business School, where he has run workshops on managing strategic change, entrepreneurship, corporate entrepreneurship, leadership, building high performance teams and sales. In addition, he has acted as course director and provided facilitation and mentoring support to participants in small groups and on a one-to-one basis.

David is a Freeman of the Guild of Entrepreneurs. He holds a Bachelor's and a Master's degree from the University of Cambridge, and is a Certified PRISM Brain Mapping Practitioner.

From Crew to Captain

A LIST OF LISTS

Book 1

by David Mellor

with illustrations by James Mellor

Published by Filament Publishing Ltd
16 Croydon Road, Waddon, Croydon,
Surrey, CR0 4PA, United Kingdom
Telephone +44(0)20 8688 2598
info@filamentpublishing.com
www.filamentpublishing.com

A List of Lists by David Mellor (Book 1)
ISBN 978-1-912635-38-2
© 2019 David Mellor

Printed by 4edge Ltd.

A quick word from David Mellor....

The purpose of this little book is to help people understand the work they will need to do in order to set up their own business. I have made this journey myself, and helped many other people do the same over almost 20 years.

I have selected 10 key areas of business start-up, and given you 10 areas to consider if you are going to move forward with confidence and "eyes wide open".

I hope that the lists will help to inform your reflection, planning and resultant activity.

If the lists create a desire to dive deeper on some of the topics, then I would encourage you do obtain a copy of my first book, *From Crew to Captain*.

Follow the link to secure your copy!
www.davidmellormentoring.com

If alternatively, or in addition, you would like to meet with me, then please let me know. You can either email me on david@davidmellormentoring.com or call me on 07957 480460.

Speed Dial

The "Speed Dial" Option

- Should I even be doing this? Jump to pages 15, 17 and 19

- What business skills will I need? Jump to page 21

- What does a business plan include? Jump to page 23

- What do I do if I need cash? Jump to page 25

- What's marketing all about? Jump to page 27

- I'm not sure about selling? Jump to page 29

- What are the most important things I need to know? Jump to page 33

A List of Lists - Contents

"You need to go into your new business venture 'eyes wide open', as opposed to 'eyes wide shut'."

Motivators

- **Personal Interest** – doing something you like or are passionate about.
- **Direct reward for efforts** – you take the risk, so you deserve the reward.
- **Flexibility** – you can influence how you spend your work and leisure time (work/life balance) and as a result can have a direct impact on your quality of life.
- **Control your own destiny** – it's your plan!
- **Own boss** – you make the rules; what is more, you can live out your personal code of conduct in the workplace.
- **Financial control** – you have a vice-like grip on cash in and out of the business.
- **No politics** – you have an opportunity to be free from politically-charged work environments.
- **Exploiting a gap in the market** – it doesn't happen often, but it is an alternative to doing something that is done already, but better or differently.
- **Fulfilment** – proving to yourself and to the market that your business idea works is a great feeling.
- **Fun** – now there's a scary concept... being paid to have fun.

"A sailor who sets off without a destination cannot possibly hope for a favourable wind."

Personal Attributes

- **Personable** – people are more likely to do business with someone where they sense a rapport.
- **Good listener** – you need to listen, and listen authentically, particularly at the various stages of the sales process.
- **Streetwise** – understanding how the small business world functions, both in general and in your part of it.
- **Discerning** – having the power of judgement in terms of decision-making, particularly regarding people.
- **Self-aware** – understanding yourself, leveraging your strengths, and working on your behavioural "blind spots".
- **Someone of integrity** – are you consistent in your behaviour with the marketplace?
- **Passionate** – if you can't be passionate about your business, don't expect anyone else to be.
- **Visionary** – can you picture in your mind's eye what you want your business to look like?
- **Confident** – have you the self-belief that you can turn your vision into a reality?
- **Determined** – are you 100% committed to giving your plan your best shot?

"Treat others like you expect to be treated."

Self-Diagnostic 1
Are you finished with your reflection phase?

ISSUE
1. Are you comfortable with not having a regular predictable salary?
2. Have you worked out your survival budget?
3. Are you confident you can exceed your survival budget?
4. Are your family supportive of your plans?
5. Have you taken sufficient advice on your idea?
6. Do you have a vision of what you want your business to look like?
7. Do you have the self-belief that you can make that vision a reality?
8. Do you have the drive and determination to make it happen?
9. Are you passionate about your idea?
10. Has anyone stress-tested your business plan for viability?

Mark yourself out of 10 for each item, and then total your score

Score < 30	You may want to rethink whether this is for you.
Score < 60	You may want to revisit some of these issues before you make a go/no-go decision.
Score > 60	You probably have enough momentum to proceed to the planning phase.

"If you work hard enough on the right things, you will make your own luck."

Business Skills Inventory

- **Technical** – do you understand the market you are planning to enter?
- **IT** – unless you are "tech savvy", find a good IT support company
- **Financial** – bookkeeping, invoicing, cash management, tax, budgeting, national insurance.
- **Sales** – do you know how to turn a stranger into cash in the bank?
- **Marketing** – can you identify people with a specific need, reach them, and then get them to like you, trust you and buy from you?
- **Networking** – an opportunity to build relationships which will lead to business over time.
- **Planning** – you need a map and a route to help you on your business journey.
- **Communication** – can you articulate your message both verbally and in writing... and can you listen authentically?
- **Time management** – you want to control the business, not have it controlling you.
- **Procurement** – have you any experience in business as a buyer?

"Look in the mirror, and make sure you know what you can and can't do; then surround yourself with quality."

Business Plan

- **Component 1** – where is the business today?

- **Component 2** – what is the product or service?

- **Component 3** – what is the market/sector?

- **Component 4** – how will you reach it?

- **Component 5** – who are you competing with?

- **Component 6** – how will the product/service be produced/created?

- **Component 7** – who are the people involved in the business?

- **Component 8** – what are the financial projections (and the assumptions behind them)?

- **Component 9** – how will the business be funded?

- **Component 10** – what are the risks (and how can they be mitigated)?

"The nice thing about not planning is that failure comes as a complete and utter surprise and isn't preceded by long periods of anguish, worry and self-doubt."

Fundraising Options

- **Family and friends** – sometimes adjusted to "The 3 Fs" (Family, Friends and Fools).
- **Overdraft** – would work for timing differences in cash flow; may need to be secured.
- **Savings** – psychologically, it increases your commitment if you risk your own capital rather than someone else's.
- **Angel equity** – prepare for a lot of networking and meetings.
- **Re-mortgage** – as per savings above, risking your own money, but make sure your partner is 100% onside with this funding strategy.
- **Grants** – vary significantly based on a) where you live and b) where you operate.
- **Secured bank loan** – would work as an alternative to angel equity
- **Crowdfunding** – worth considering, has worked for many. Take a look at invoice discounting which operates well through crowdfunding routes.
- **Credit cards** – really only worth considering as an alternative to overdraft i.e. to cover short-term timing differences.
- **Business partners and/or customers** – the former may help as an extra pair of hands as well as a source of cash, but be very careful with choice of person and financial terms; the latter may well depend on how important your product or service is to the customer in question.

"Remember that financiers will not be comfortable funding your lifestyle."

Marketing

- **Question 1** – What problem are you solving?
- **Question 2** – Who faces this problem?
- **Question 3** – Is the market big and attractive enough to generate sufficient profits?
- **Question 4** – How attractive is the industry in terms of competition?
- **Question 5** – How do you reach the audience?
- **Question 6** – What will your marketing mix need to be?
- **Question 7** – Is your branding and messaging consistent across all client touchpoints?
- **Question 8** – Is it also clear, concise and jargon-free?
- **Question 9** – Do you understand how the buying process works?
- **Question 10** – Have you created a value proposition?

"Ready, Fire, Aim doesn't work, but people keep trying."

Sales

- Listen (and listen authentically).
- It's all about the client/prospect, not about you (enter their world, rather than drag them in to yours).
- Build the relationship (and the trust that goes with it).
- Research (get to know your prospect well).
- Be determined (but not desperate).
- Sales qualification is a two-way process (not all clients are good clients).
- Never get complacent (and never "wing it").
- It's all about the why (be clear on where you add value and what problems you solve).
- Choose your moment (prospect needs to be in buying mode for you to be able to sell).
- Learn to discern when a lead is going nowhere ("yes" or "no" is better than "maybe").

"You know you have made it when the prospect wants to buy from you rather than you having to sell to them."

Self-Diagnostic 2

1. Have you completed a business skills inventory?
2. Have you worked out a training/resourcing plan based on the inventory?
3. Have you defined what success will look like for you?
4. Have you fully researched the market?
5. Have you created some basic sales and delivery processes?
6. Have you established your cost base?
7. Do you have a revenue model?
8. Have you identified a mentor?
9. Have you profiled your clients?
10. Have you identified and analysed your competition?

Mark yourself out of 10 for each item, and then total your score

Score < 30   You may be embarking on your business "eyes wide shut"! More homework may be required.

Score < 60   You may want to spend some more time preparing for launch.

Score > 60   You probably have enough momentum to proceed to the launch phase.

"A good plan to day is better than a perfect plan tomorrow."

Top Tips

- **Look in the mirror** – capitalise on your self-awareness; leverage and mitigate weaknesses.
- **Find a mentor** – he/she can help combat loneliness and act as a sounding board regarding attitude, mindset and business ideas.
- **Surround yourself with quality** – don't compromise on business partners, associates, staff or service providers.
- **Launch "eyes wide open"** – make sure you know what you are getting into.
- **Work on your personal brand** – make sure it is consistent and coherent across all touchpoints.
- **Understand your financial drivers** – margins, break-even, liquidity, debtors.
- **Work to a plan with simple performance metrics** - where are you going, and how will you get there.
- **Learn the art of networking** – how to build rapport, trust and relationships; "be interested not interesting".
- **Develop your communication skills** – written and verbal. Don't forget to listen.
- **Never stop investing** in your own personal development.

"You don't want to end up like Christopher Columbus, who when he set off didn't know where he was going, when he got there he didn't know where he was, and when he got back he didn't know where he'd been, and he did all of this with someone else's money."

FROM CREW TO CAPTAIN (Book 1)
Making the transition from working for a big institution
to working for yourself
By David Mellor
with original illustrations by James Mellor

The purpose of this book is to help people understand the transition from working for a big institution to working for themselves. I have made this journey, and helped many others do the same. I want to put the odds in your favour, if you decide to follow suit, that your business venture brings you everything you wish, and that you prosper rather than merely survive. You will find inside a number of practical tips and hints, all garnered from the "University of Life".

I will draw on a broad range of interview material from people who have made or are making this journey, and for whom success has looked very different. It will also draw on a wealth of anecdotal evidence, from my own experience and that of others.

Our journey will take us through three important phases:

1. Reflecting - what does it take to make this transition - and is it for you?

2. Planning - how do you go about preparing to launch your business?

3. Doing - what attributes are going to be really important in the early days post launch?

www.davidmellormentoring.com

FROM CREW TO CAPTAIN: A PRIVATEER'S TALE (Book 2)
by David Mellor
with original illustrations by James Mellor

The user-friendly guide to launching and growing a successful consultancy business

When you're launching your own business, there's nothing like friendly, straightforward advice to set you on the right course. My book *From Crew To Captain: A Privateer's Tale* takes sound business advice and delivers it in a jargon-free, conversational style, making it that rarest of beasts: a business book that is both informative and enjoyable to read!

As a consultant and mentor, since 2001 I have helped scores of people successfully launch their own business. My first book, *From Crew To Captain*, guided aspiring entrepreneurs through the transition from being part of a big institution to working for themselves.

From Crew To Captain: A Privateer's Tale is designed to help people take the next steps of their journey as they launch and, with any luck, grow their new practice. This easy-to-absorb advice and tips are interspersed with useful checklists and light-hearted illustrations as well as one or two cautionary anecdotes!

Drawing from my own successful career as a consultant and through interviews with colleagues, peers and mentees, *From Crew To Captain: A Privateer's Tale* delivers honest, pragmatic advice and offers a simple but highly effective framework that will help consultants from almost any sector maximise their chances of developing a profitable, successful business.

This book is for you if...

- you are contemplating, or in the process of, a career change, be it planned or enforced.

- you would like to make money out of what you have learned in your career to date.

- you want to understand how to set up a sole practitioner consultancy practice or similar.

- you don't know what you don't know in terms of making the transition successfully.

- you would like to know more about what "good consultancy" looks like.

- you need help in addressing how to sell consultancy services.

- you are keen to achieve "client delight" through your delivery.

- you would welcome someone going on the journey with you.

FROM CREW TO CAPTAIN: COMMANDER OF THE FLEET (Book 3)
by David Mellor
with original illustrations by James Mellor

This book completes a trilogy. Book 1 (*From Crew to Captain*) addressed how to make the transition from working for a big institution to working for yourself. Book 2 (*A Privateer's Tale*) looked specifically at how to set up as a sole practitioner consultant or similar.

The purpose of this book is to help people who have set up their own business, proved to themselves and the market that their model works, and are looking to take it to the next level. I have made this journey, and helped many others do the same.

As with the first two books, you will find inside a number of practical tips and hints, all garnered from the "University of Life".

We will look at 4 important aspects of early business growth:

1. Assessing the Situation - what does the business look like today, and why do you want to change it?

2. Achieving Transformation - how do you go about creating and implementing a change strategy?

3. Assessing the Outcome – how do you evaluate success?

4. Building a Consultancy Practice – how do you move from a sole practitioner to a multi-consultant practice?

You may be wondering why I decided to put pen to paper again having written the first two books. One of the issues, which is important to me, is closure. I don't like loose ends, and I had a sense that the first two books left some "unfinished business". I knew I wouldn't rest easy until I had dealt with it by writing Book 3.

So, this book picks up the journey from where the first two books left off. My personal sub-title for the book is "Growing pains and how to deal with them", because that is exactly what the book addresses. Whatever type of business you are trying to build, I hope you will find some "gold nuggets" there.

This book is for you if...

- you have an existing business.

- you have proved to yourself and the market that your business model works.

- you want to understand how to take the business to the next level.

- you don't know what you don't know in terms of making the transition successfully.

- you would like to know more about how to create a value business capable of sustainable profitable growth.

- as a specific issue, you need help in addressing how you move from a sole practitioner model to running a multi-consultant practice.

- you would welcome someone going on the journey with you.